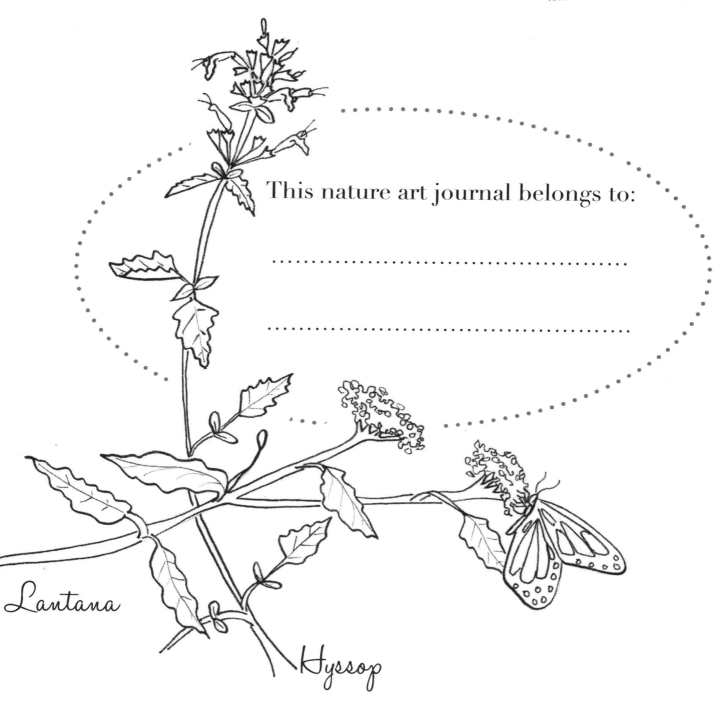

This nature art journal belongs to:

....

....

Lantana

Hyssop

Wings, Worms, and Wonder 12 Month Art & Nature Journal
©Kelly Johnson 2016

ISBN 978-1537703176

Published by Wings ,Worms, and Wonder
Neptune Beach, Florida
www.wingswormsandwonder.com

Printed by Createspace Publishing

**The paper in this journal works best with pencils & color pencils.
If using markers, to prevent bleed through,
place a blank sheet of cardstock between pages.**

Wings, Worms, and Wonder

12 Month Art & Nature Journal

Mindfully Color, Sketch, & Relax Your Way Into Nature

By Kelly Johnson

Welcome!

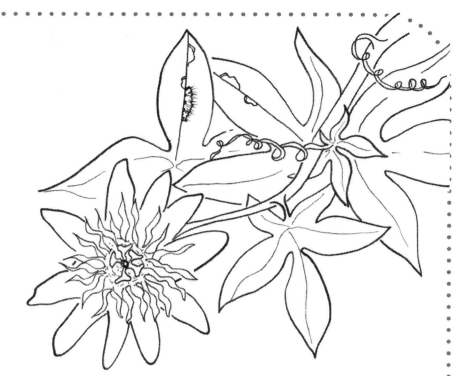

I'm so glad you're here!
This is your place to connect with
the wonders of the natural world,
creatively!

Simply follow where your sense
of wonder leads you – near or far,
from a beautiful bowl of produce,
to a potted house plant, to the backyard, to a local garden or park, & into the forest wilds.
No nature is too big or small when we listen for Mother Nature's whispers & wonders!

A Few Suggestions:

There is no right or wrong way to use this nature art journal, so start with your Creative
Connection Intention & then jump in anywhere – color the passiflora on this very page today!
At the end of 12 months, you'll have a beautiful journal full of your creative nature
connections. Draw, sketch, collage, & creatively connect everywhere. There's lots of open space
& even pages in the back for: Reflections, Notes, Further Explorations, Sketching, & Coloring!

Also, consider dating your creations in the extra idea space at the bottom of each page. It's fun
to reminisce once your journal is full & dates help you track your nature observations.

Each month offers you: 5 free pages for you to clear your mind & journal your connections
however you like, A coloring & sketching prompt page, A flower symbolism coloring page, &
A daily thumbnail sketch page where you can make a teeny connection each day of the month.
These pages are full of creative connecting possibility, so experiment – color, sketch, & add
your own details inside the lines & out! It's your art & nature journal, so let loose!

Creative Nature Connection Intention

Express in pictures, words, or collage any intentions you'd like to make as you begin your 12 month creative nature connection journey.

"One way to open your eyes to
unnoticed beauty is to ask yourself,

'What if I had never seen this before?
What if I knew I would
never see it again?'"

Rachel Carson

Decorate this quote. Observe & sketch nearby nature that sparks your sense of wonder.

January

Snowdrop

(Galanthus nivalis)
Hope & Rebirth

Sunday	Monday	Tuesday	Wednesday	Thursday	Friday	Saturday

Monthly
Explorations & Ephemera

Twists & turns make life interesting!
Plumeria flowers bloom from a spiral,
creatively explore twist and turns you
observe in nature.

February

Primrose

(Primula) Patience, Kindness, & Gentleness

Sunday	Monday	Tuesday	Wednesday	Thursday	Friday	Saturday

Monthly
Explorations & Ephemera

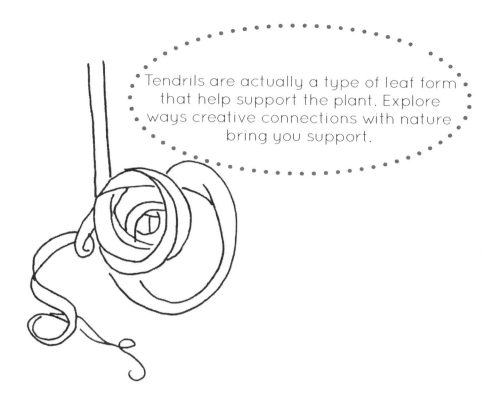

Tendrils are actually a type of leaf form that help support the plant. Explore ways creative connections with nature bring you support.

March

Daffodil

(Narcissus pseudonarcissus)
Creativity & Inspiration

Sunday	Monday	Tuesday	Wednesday	Thursday	Friday	Saturday

Monthly
Explorations & Ephemera

Spring brings sprouts! Design a nature filled space where you can sprout your creative connections! Maybe it's a veggie or butterfly garden, a labyrinth, or maybe it's something from your inspired imagination!

Gerber Daisy

(Gerbera jamesonii)
Truth & Happiness

April

Sunday	Monday	Tuesday	Wednesday	Thursday	Friday	Saturday

Monthly
Explorations & Ephemera

Consider your observations of flowers, then invent your own varieties here!

May

Hawthorne

(Crataegus)
Balance & Duality

Sunday	Monday	Tuesday	Wednesday	Thursday	Friday	Saturday

Monthly
Explorations & Ephemera

Add more vines, flowers & pods to the pea!

Honeysuckle

(Lonicera japonica)
United in Love & Devotion

June

Sunday	Monday	Tuesday	Wednesday	Thursday	Friday	Saturday

Monthly
Explorations & Ephemera

From wild natives to planned plantings, creatively express 3 nature discoveries. (This is a mum, expressed in a fun style.)

July

Larkspur

(Consolida)
Lightness, Laughter, & Love

Sunday	Monday	Tuesday	Wednesday	Thursday	Friday	Saturday

Monthly
Explorations & Ephemera

Like grape vines grow with vigor, what edibles would you like to grow or forage if given the opportunity?

August

Gladiolus

(Gladiolus)
Sincerity & Integrity

Sunday	Monday	Tuesday	Wednesday	Thursday	Friday	Saturday

Monthly
Explorations & Ephemera

Ginger flowers smell so sweet. How could you express the smells of nature visually? Try abstract color explorations, representational forms, or even collage with real nature items!

Aster

(Asteraceae)
Patience & Elegance

September

Sunday	Monday	Tuesday	Wednesday	Thursday	Friday	Saturday

Monthly
Explorations & Ephemera

Create a design inspired by the ways seeds blow through the wind. Even try inventing your own types of seeds!

October

Marigold

(Tagetes)
Remembrance &
Promoting Cheer

Sunday	Monday	Tuesday	Wednesday	Thursday	Friday	Saturday

Monthly
Explorations & Ephemera

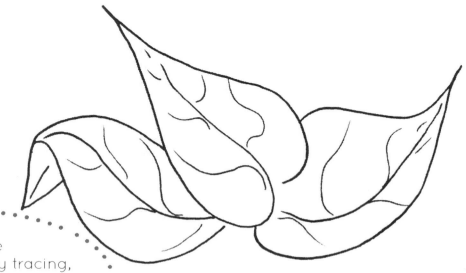

Explore the
textures of leaves by tracing,
sketching, & making rubbings from
leaves you collect.

November

Chrysanthemum

(Dendranthema)
Support Endurance, & Loyalty

Sunday	Monday	Tuesday	Wednesday	Thursday	Friday	Saturday

Monthly
Explorations & Ephemera

The acorn doesn't fall far from the tree,
or so the saying goes.
Do you find that to be true, or do you
sprout a new style of nature connected
life?
Explore your roots & seeds creatively.

December

Narcissus

(Narcissus)
Respect,
Good Luck,
& Prosperity

Sunday	Monday	Tuesday	Wednesday	Thursday	Friday	Saturday

Monthly
Explorations & Ephemera

Euphorbia grow & bloom in extremes.
How does a creative connection with
nature support your growth & blooming
through extremes & transitions?

Creative Nature Connection Reflections

Express in pictures, words, or collage special reflections, observations, inspirations, & discoveries about your connection experiences over your 12 month creative nature connection journey.

Spontaneous Sketches

Thoughts, Discoveries, & Ideas to Further Explore

Notes

About the Author

Kelly Johnson is an artist, author, & creative nature connection guide helping connect the world to nature through her little company Wings, Worms, and Wonder. That's me!

I truly believe that the arts are a fantastically powerful tool to keep humans connected to the wonders of our natural world in the fast paced modern life. To my work, I bring a BFA, an MA in Environmental Studies, an AMS Montessori teaching credential, & perhaps most importantly, a lifetime of loving art, nature, gardening, & the peace of creative connection.

Through my books, online courses & classes, art, workshops, presentations, & blog, I (Kelly) hope to inspire & give humans of all ages the opportunity to bring more joy, peace, & mindful relaxation into their lives through the process of creative nature connection & nature journaling.

For More

Head over to my website & shop for more tips, tools, resources, & inspiration to keep you creatively connecting with nature all year long!

Bottlebrush

While you're there, check out my:
Online nature art journaling eClasses & eCourses
(there's even a free one!), More books (including coloring books),
Fun nature journaling art accessories (stickers, prints, pencil pouches, fun!)
& Be sure to Subscribe to my newsletter to get VIP discounts, sale info,
+ free monthly creative nature connection activities delivered right to you!

wingswormsandwonder.com

Follow & Share @ wingswormsandwonder

Additional Titles by Kelly

Wings, Worms, and Wonder:
A Guide for Creatively Integrating Gardening and Outdoor
Learning Into Children's Lives

The Wings, Worms, and Wonder
Nature Journal Prompt Cards

12 Months of Wonder Wednesday Activities eBook

Flora of Fun: Flower Symbolism of Fun, Friendship, &
Lightheartedness Mini Coloring Book

Find These & More:

etsy.com/shop/WingsWormsAndWonder

"What the hand does, the mind remembers."

Maria Montessori

Creatively connecting doesn't stop here. You have the inspiration & the nature journal practice.

May your peace, joy, & creative nature connections keep flowing throughout life's seasons!

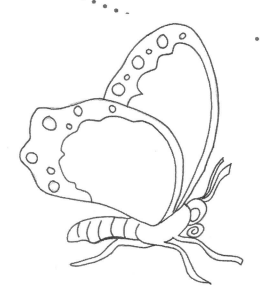

Nature Journal eCourses with Kelly

Grow your nature journal practice with a
Wings, Worms, and Wonder Nature Journaling eCourse!

Expand your drawing & painting skills, deepen creative
nature experiences with nature connection meditations,
explore color theory for nature journalers, discover a little
ethnobotany, & lots more!

All within a supportive creative nature loving community!

All experience levels welcome!

Learn More
& Take a Free Class:

wings-worms-and-wonder-classroom.teachable.com

Thank You!

Wild Iris
A Message

Ferm
Sincerity

Wild Angelica
Inspiration

Made in the USA
Lexington, KY
18 March 2017